Written and compiled by Todd Hafer.

ISBN 978-1-61626-638-7

Cover and interior design: Kirk DouPonce, DogEared Design
Cover and interior illustrations: Jody Williams

Published by Barbour Publishing, Inc., P.O. Box 719, Uhrichsville, Ohio 44683, www.barbourbooks.com

Our mission is to publish and distribute inspirational products offering exceptional value and biblical encouragement to the masses.

Member of the
Evangelical Christian
Publishers Association

Printed in India.

I will wait on the LORD . . .
And I will hope in Him.
Here am I and the children
whom the LORD has given me!

ISAIAH 8:17–18

Mom, you're

mah-velous!

because...

you listen—*really* listen—
to everything on my heart.

Mom, you're

mah-velous!

because...

if patience is a virtue,
you're already a saint!

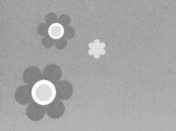

Mom, you're

mah-velous!

because...

you've always believed in me—
even when I've doubted myself.

Mom, you're

mah-velous!

because...

you always know just what I need—
even when I don't have a clue.

Mom, you're

mah-velous!

because...

my heart remembers every
hug and kiss you ever gave me.

Mom, you're

mah-velous!

because...

you've taught me that God's
way can be my way, too!

We find a delight in the beauty
and happiness of children that makes
the heart too big for the body.

RALPH WALDO EMERSON

Mom, you're

mah-velous!

because...

you can bring peace to even the
most heated family squabble.

Mom, you're

mah-velous!

because...

you know the difference between
the house being quiet and the
house being *too* quiet.

Mom, you're

mah-velous!

because...

when I'm with you,
I feel completely loved.

Mom, you're

mah-velous!

because...

you always know when to hang on,
and when to let go.

Mom, you're

mah-velous!

because...

you've taught me to be an original *me*—
not a copy of someone else.

Mom, you're

mah-veloüs!

because...

you can multitask like nobody's business!

All that I am, all I ever hope to be,
I owe to my angel mother.

ABRAHAM LINCOLN

Mom, you're

mah-velous!

because...

inside your hug is one of the
best places in the world.

Mom, you're

mah-velous!

because...

you know that the shortest
words can speak volumes.

Mom, you're

mah-velous!

because...

you can listen to three people talking
at the same time—and comprehend
everything they're saying!

Mom, you're

mah-velous!

because...

you've fought a lot of battles for me—
but also encouraged me to fight
many other battles for myself.

Mom, you're

mah-velous!

because...

when you say "I'm so proud of you!"
I know you really mean it.

Mom, you're

mah-velous!

because...

you taught me that seatbelts,
showers, and cruciferous vegetables
can all be my friends!

Even when I couldn't understand my
mother's words, I understood her love.

OLIVIA KENT

Mom, you're

mah-velous!

because...

you know I need love the most
when I deserve it the least!

Mom, you're

mah-velous!

because...

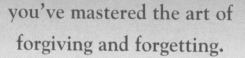

you've mastered the art of
forgiving and forgetting.

Mom, you're

mah-velous!

because...

you know that true love means letting
someone else choose the pizza toppings.

Mom, you're

mah-velous!

because...

time after time your support has
made all the difference in the world!

Mom, you're

mah-velous!

because...

you keep your promises.

Mom, you're

mah-velous!

because...

you've taught me that true happiness
isn't in things, it's in *us*.

The woman is the heart of the home.

<small>MOTHER TERESA</small>

Mom, you're

mah-velous!

because...

your eyes still light up when
you look at the people you love.

Mom, you're

mah-velous!

because...

I know you pray for me all the time.

Mom, you're

mah-velous!

because...

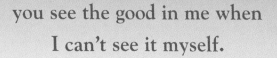

you see the good in me when
I can't see it myself.

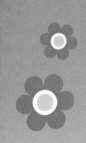

Mom, you're

mah-velous!

because...

your laugh is one of the
happiest sounds in my world!

Mom, you're

mah-velous!

because...

even though you're always busy,
you're never too busy for me!

Mom, you're

mah-velous!

because...

you're the maestro of the microwave!

A mother could perform the jobs of several air-traffic controllers with ease.

LISA ALTHER

Mom, you're

mah-velous!

because...

you've shown me that a woman can
be gentle and yet strong.

Mom, you're

mah-velous!

because...

you can think "on the fly"
like no one else I know!

Mom, you're

mah-velous!

because...

you love me just the way I am.

Mom, you're

mah-velous!

because...

you have turned so many of my
failures into successes.

Mom, you're

mah-velous!

because...

I can always count on you
for an honest answer.

Mom, you're

mah-velous!

because...

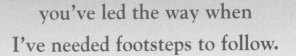

you've led the way when
I've needed footsteps to follow.

So sweet and precious is family life.

JAMES McBRIDE

Mom, you're

mah-velous!

because...

you've walked behind me when
I needed some gentle prodding.

Mom, you're

mah-velous!

because...

you've walked beside me when
I needed a friend.

Mom, you're

mah-velous!

because...

you know that where there's smoke. . .
there's Dad, trying to cook something.

Mom, you're

mah-velous!

because...

you taught me that healthful foods aren't as bad-tasting as their reputation suggests!

Mom, you're

mah-velous!

because...

you love me the way only a mother can.

Mom, you're

mah-velous!

because...

you wear so many hats. . .
Doctor
Financial advisor
Beautician
Fashion policewoman
Counselor
Dietician
Friend

One of the luckiest things that can happen to you in life is to have a happy childhood.

AGATHA CHRISTIE

Mom, you're

mah-velous!

because...

even when we're miles apart,
you can still make me feel "hugged."

Mom, you're

mah-velous!

because...

you've taught me life lessons by what
you say and, more importantly,
by who you are.

Mom, you're

mah-velous!

because...

you've waited for me—
and waited *on* me—when anyone else's
patience would have run dry.

Mom, you're

mah-velous!

because...

you're my own
personal Super Woman!

Mom, you're

mah-velous!

because...

you look at me and see a miracle
when everyone else sees a mess.

Mom, you're

mah-velous!

because...

time after time your wisdom
has kept me on the right path.

Hold tenderly that which you cherish.

BOB ALBERT

Mom, you're

mah-velous!

because...

your love has always been there when
I need it. (And I'll *always* need it.)

Mom, you're

mah-velous!

because...

no one does comfort food like you.

Mom, you're

mah-velous!

because...

you lighten my burdens by sharing them.

Mom, you're

mah-velous!

because...

you have the strength to move
mountains—and I don't mean just
the mountains of laundry!

Mom, you're

mah-velous!

because...

you're my own personal
rainbow on stormy days.

Mom, you're

mah-velous!

because...

you love me as I am—but you also
want me to be all that I can be.

Her eyes are homes of silent prayer.

Mom, you're

mah-velous!

because...

I smile when I catch myself quoting
some of your words of wisdom.

Mom, you're

mah-velous!

because...

many of the things I like best
about myself are also things
I like best about you!

Mom, you're

mah-velous!

because...

you've taught me that life's most
beautiful things cannot be seen;
they must be felt with the heart.

Mom, you're

mah-velous!

because...

an outing with you is more fun
than a trip to an amusement park.

Mom, you're

mah-veloüs!

because...

you've taught me that two of the
most powerful words in the
English language are "thank you."

Mom, you're

mah-velous!

because...

your supply of hugs and kisses
seems to be endless!

If you want a happy family,
if you want a holy family,
give your hearts to love.

MOTHER TERESA

Mom, you're

mah-velous!

because...

you've taught me that laughter is
contagious—but so is the flu!

Mom, you're

mah-velous!

because...

you've taught me that fashion
can be purchased, but true style
must be developed.

Mom, you're

mah-velous!

because...

you were my role model when
everyone else was my critic.

Mom, you're

mah-velous!

because…

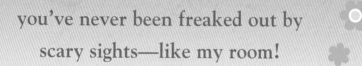

you've never been freaked out by
scary sights—like my room!

Mom, you're

mah-velous!

because...

you've taught me that well-done
is better than well-said.

Mom, you're

mah-velous!

because...

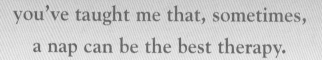

you've taught me that, sometimes,
a nap can be the best therapy.

Mom, you're

mah-velous!

because...

you've taught me that
"humble pie" is health food.

Oh, what a power
is motherhood.

EURIPIDES